Fast and Slow

Color the fast animals.
Circle the slow animals.

Turtle

Rabbit

Dog

Snail

Worm

Cheetah

Horse

Starfish

Few and Many

Draw lines to match the images.

FEW   **MANY**

Big and Small

Which animal is big?
Color the small animal.

Mouse

Elephant

Which one in the picture is small?
Color the tree.

Tree

Plant

Color the bigger picture.
Circle the small picture.

Star

Sun

Which dog is small?
Color the big dog.

St. Bernard

Chihuahua

Color the bigger picture.
Circle the small picture.

Building

House

Clean and Dirty

Draw a line to match the opposite pictures.
Color the clean pictures.

Cross out the objects that are dirty.
Color the objects that are clean.

Healthy and Sick

Draw a line to match the opposite pictures.

Healthy   Sick

Light and Heavy

Match the objects by drawing a line. Color the pictures that are heavier.

Match the objects by drawing a line.
Color the pictures that are heavier.

Color the correct picture for each sentence.

The man is old.

The girl is young.

The nurse is happy.

The policeman is sad.

The cow is fat.

The dog is thin.

The cup is full.

The bottle is empty.

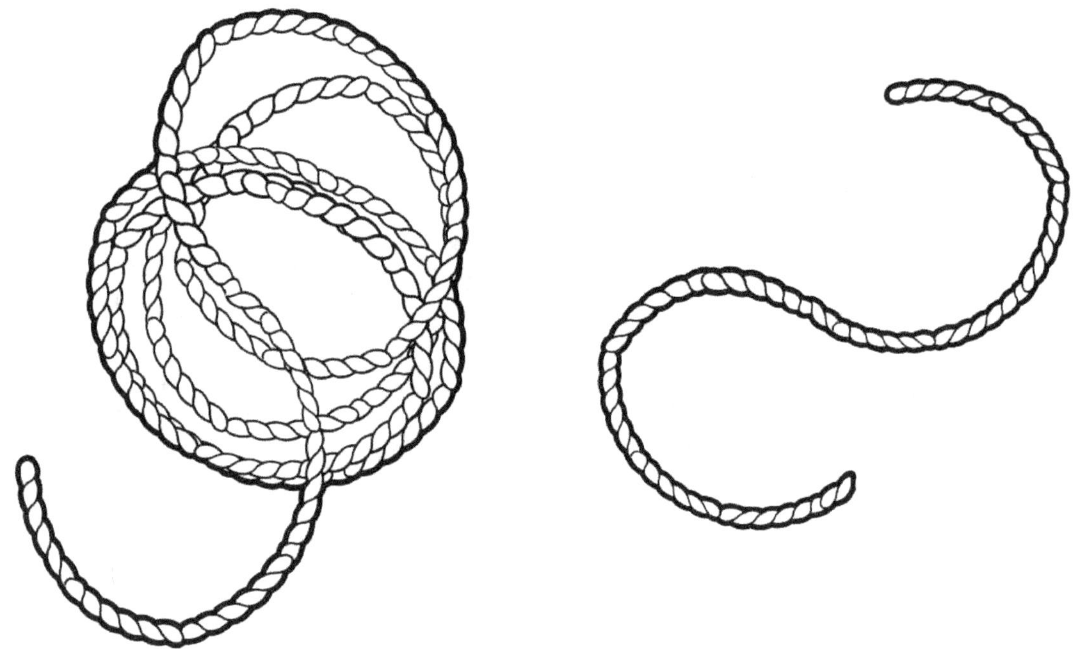

The rope is long.

The skirt is short.

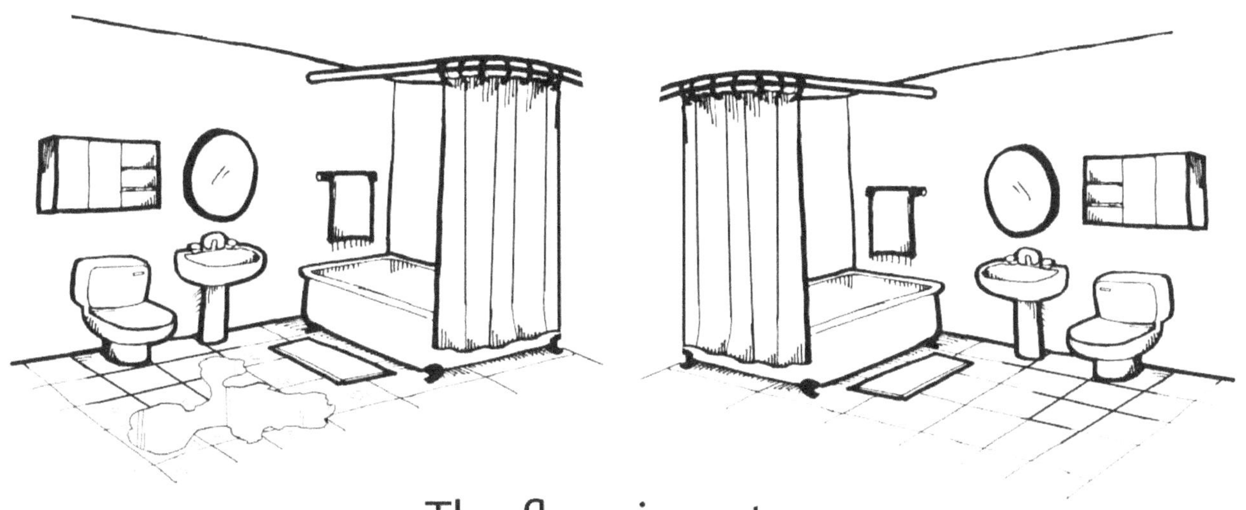

The floor is wet.

The towel is dry.

Hard and Soft

Which objects are hard? ✔

Which objects are soft? ✘

Tall and Short

Who is tall? Put a check. 

Who is short? Put a cross. 

Color the tall boy.

Near and Far

Which animals are near Jack?
Color the animals that are far
from Jack.